★ *GREAT SPORTS TEAMS* ★

THE NEW YORK

HOCKEY TEAM

Michael J. Sullivan

 Enslow Publishers, Inc.

44 Fadem Road   PO Box 38
Box 699   Aldershot
Springfield, NJ 07081   Hants GU12 6BP
USA   UK

Library of Congress Cataloging-in-Publication Data

Sullivan, Michael John, 1960–
    The New York Rangers hockey team / Michael J. Sullivan.
        p. cm. — (Great sports teams)
    Includes bibliographical references (p.) and index.
    Summary: Surveys the key personalities and games in the history of the New York Rangers hockey team, focusing on the 1994 Stanley Cup championship.
    ISBN 0-7660-1023-6
    1. New York Rangers (Hockey team)—History—Juvenile literature. 2. Stanley Cup (Hockey)—Juvenile literature. [1. New York Rangers (Hockey team)—History. 2. Hockey—History.] I. Title. II. Series.
GV848.N43S85 1998
796.96′264′097471—dc21   97-21310
                                                                     CIP
                                                                      AC

Printed in the United States of America

10 9 8 7 6 5 4 3 2 1

Illustration Credits: AP/Wide World Photos, pp. 4, 7, 8, 10, 13, 14, 16, 19, 20, 22, 25, 26, 28, 31, 32, 34, 37, 38.

Cover Illustration: AP/Wide World Photos.

CONTENTS

J eff Beukeboom of the New York Rangers checks Greg Adams of the Vancouver Canucks. The Rangers and Canucks battled for the 1994 Stanley Cup championship.

THE DROUGHT IS OVER

There was excitement in New York City for the first time in many decades when discussing hockey late in the 1993–94 season. The Rangers had made it to the Stanley Cup Finals. The Rangers hadn't won a Stanley Cup in fifty-four years—a long time. A very long time, indeed, for the Rangers fans.

Vancouver stunned the Rangers in Game 1, winning in overtime on the Rangers' home ice. Then, New York bounced back in Games 2, 3, and 4. It appeared that the Rangers were ready to grab the Stanley Cup on their home ice in Game 5. Before a roaring crowd thirsty to drink from the Cup, the Rangers disappointed themselves and the fans by losing. To make matters even worse, New York saw the series tied at three games apiece when the Canucks won Game 6 on Vancouver's home ice.

It was horrible to think that the Rangers may lose Game 7. A crowd of 18,200 gathered at Madison Square Garden on June 14, 1994. New York wanted to get its home crowd into the game early so scoring the first goal was very important.

After a shot by the Canucks Pavel Bure, Rangers defenseman Brian Leetch picked up the puck by the Rangers' net. Leetch snapped a pass off the right boards toward a streaking Mark Messier. Messier picked up the puck by the boards and crossed over the blue line. He eyed Canucks goalie Kirk McLean, but the shot on goal would have been difficult. Messier was at a sharp angle to the net. Messier stopped and started skating toward the center. The crowd started to roar, sensing something special might happen.

Messier looked around to see what his best option was—shoot or pass. Messier spotted defenseman Sergei Zubov circling around his right side and heading toward the net. Messier made a beautiful behind-the-back pass to Zubov, who quickly passed it to Leetch, standing to the left of McLean. Leetch fired! He scored! The Rangers led 1–0! The crowd at the Garden roared. Messier and Leetch celebrated by hugging each other.

The Rangers continued to forecheck and work hard at trying to get the puck along the boards. Their hard work paid off. Referee Terry Gregson called Jyrki Lumme of the Canucks for holding. This gave the Rangers a power play. Coach Mike Keenan immediately sent out Messier's line for more offense. Shots by Leetch and Alexei Kovalev were stopped by

*A*dam Graves (9) looks to push the puck past Capitals defenseman Calle Johansson and goalie Jim Hrivnak. Graves scored the second goal in Game 7 of the 1994 Cup finals.

McLean. Yet the pressure from the Rangers' power play continued to mount.

Kovalev moved across the left side and had Adam Graves in the middle. Messier was stationed to the right of Graves. Kovalev passed to Graves, who shot quickly. Goal! The Rangers now led 2–0!

Messier and the Rangers realized they could not relax. There was still plenty of time remaining. The Canucks Greg Adams came speeding down the center toward Rangers goalie Mike Richter. Adams shot, and the puck slipped through Richter . . . but dribbled wide of the net! New York still led 2–0.

*F*ormer Rangers captain Mark Messier holds up the Stanley Cup in celebration as the city of New York congratulates its team.

The Canucks Come Back

In the second period, the Canucks started to apply some offensive pressure on Richter. With Gregson about to call a penalty on the Rangers, the Canucks Trevor Linden picked up a bouncing puck near center ice. He immediately turned himself around and sped toward the Rangers' net. With Leetch trying to hold him up from behind, Linden moved around the defenseman and chipped the puck over Richter's shoulder and into the net. Goal! The Canucks now trailed 2–1.

The Rangers came back. Rangers winger Brian Noonan skated toward the Canucks net and tried to pass to Graves. The Canucks defenseman had Graves pinned, so Noonan's pass deflected off of Graves and away from the pile in front.

Noonan regained the puck and took a shot toward McLean. It was stopped in front, but Messier reached out with his stick and slapped at the puck. "Goal!" The crowd roared as Messier swung his arms skyward when the light went on behind the Canucks cage to signify a score. The Rangers now led 3–1.

The Canucks started to pressure as well. Bure intercepted a Ranger's pass and darted between the Rangers' defense. When he was about to get off a shot, Rangers winger Esa Tikkanen dragged Bure down in front of Richter. A penalty was called on the Rangers. It did not take long before Linden scored again. The Rangers now led 3–2. Yet time was on the Rangers' side.

The Canucks continued to press as the clock showed 1:34 left. A shot by the Canucks was blocked in front by Messier. One minute was left. Vancouver pulled McLean out of the nets for another skater. The puck deflected up into the stands . . . 37.8 seconds left. The Canucks continued to press. Bure's shot was stopped in front . . . 1.1 seconds remained!

Pandemonium

The puck was dropped for the face-off, and deflected behind the Rangers' net. The Rangers win! The Rangers win! The drought was over! Fireworks exploded inside the fabled arena in New York City as the Rangers mobbed and hugged each other. People outside the Garden were jumping around and shouting. Messier and Coach Keenan hugged each other at center ice. The crowd was deafening. The fifty-four-year wait was over.

*S*ports promoter George "Tex" Rickard is the man most responsible for the birth of the Rangers' franchise.

THE RANGERS' STORY

The Rangers' long road to the 1994 Stanley Cup Championship began in 1926 when boxing promoter George "Tex" Rickard had an idea. Why not bring hockey to New York City? The team could play at the new Madison Square Garden, which had just been rebuilt on Eighth Avenue. Rickard quickly hired Conn Smythe, who had already managed hockey teams in Canada, to put together a new team. Sportswriters began calling the new team "Tex's Rangers."[1] The last part of the name stuck, and the New York Rangers were born.

However, Conn Smythe didn't last long. After too many disagreements with the team's management, he was replaced by Lester Patrick. Patrick's nickname was "the Silver Fox" because of his white hair. Patrick put together an amazing team. There were future Hall of Famers Frank Boucher and Bill Cook, Hall of Fame defenseman Ivan "Ching" Johnson, and winger

Murray Murdoch. Murdoch would go on to play in 508 consecutive games. He was also former Rangers' captain Mark Messier's great-uncle!

A Great Beginning

The young team played its first game on November 17, 1926. The Rangers shut out the Montreal Maroons, 1–0, with wing Bill Cook scoring the only goal.

The Rangers captured first-place in the American Division. Even though they were eliminated by the Boston Bruins in postseason play, the Rangers had made a name for themselves. Everyone wanted to see this new team play. Even baseball stars Babe Ruth and Lou Gehrig came to watch a few games![2]

In the 1927–28 season, the Rangers played even better. They defeated both Pittsburgh and Boston to gain a spot in the Finals against the Montreal Maroons. There was one problem, however. Every year, the circus came to Madison Square Garden. When it came, the Rangers were forced to play all of their "home" games in Montreal. Despite the boos of the Montreal fans, the Rangers beat the Maroons three games to two. The Rangers had won the Stanley Cup in only their second year in the league!

Over the next five years, the Rangers never finished worse than third in their division. In 1933, they competed against Toronto in the Finals. Once again, the circus was in town, and the Rangers had to play some of their home games in Canada. One year earlier, the Maple Leafs had beaten New York badly in

*T*he 1939–40 New York Rangers celebrate one of the team's victories. This team would go on to win the Stanley Cup. It would be fifty-four years before the Rangers would win another.

postseason play. This time, the Rangers had their revenge. They won the series 3–1. In seven short years, the Rangers had won the Cup twice.

This winning could not continue forever. Some of the Rangers were getting older. Lester Patrick helped create a farm club that would bring new talent onto the team. Players such as Bryan Hextall, Dutch Hiller, Alex Shibicky, Phil Watson, and Patrick's own sons, Lynn and Murray, helped the Rangers regain their winning ways. In 1940, the Rangers won their third Stanley Cup, thanks to Bryan Hextall's overtime goal against Toronto in Game 6!

R od Gilbert of the New York Rangers checks
Dennis Hull of the Chicago Black Hawks.
The Rangers Jean Ratelle looks on.

The Start of a Dry Spell

The year 1940 was to be the last championship year for a long time. Many of the best players were drafted into the military during World War II. The rest of that decade was very frustrating for both the Rangers and their fans. However, the Rangers finally qualified for postseason play in 1950. They defeated the Montreal Canadiens and went on to battle the Detroit Red Wings. It was a tough six-game series that the Rangers eventually lost, but they could be proud of their efforts.

During the 1950s and 1960s, the Rangers missed the postseason twelve times. Even if they managed to make it into the playoffs, they always lost in the first round. The fans were disappointed. It must have been especially frustrating for Lorne "Gump" Worsley, the man who played more games than any other goalie in Rangers history.

Falling Short

In 1964, Emile Francis took over as coach and began rebuilding the team. Beginning in 1966–67, the Rangers made the playoffs nine consecutive seasons. Rod Gilbert, Jean Ratelle, and Vic Hadfield were a powerful force for the Rangers. All three became All-Stars, along with defenseman Brad Park and goalie Ed Giacomin. During the 1970–71 season, the Rangers made it to the second round of the playoffs, where they lost to the great Bobby Hull and the Chicago Black Hawks. During the 1971–72 season, Vic Hadfield became the first Ranger to score 50 goals in one season. He helped lead New York to the Stanley Cup Finals against the Boston Bruins. Unfortunately, the Bruins had legendary defenseman Bobby Orr on their team, and the Rangers were defeated.

In 1979, Rangers' fans were given hope once more. New York defeated the Los Angeles Kings and Philadelphia Flyers. They then beat their crosstown enemies, the New York Islanders. Exhausted, the Rangers fell in the Finals to the Montreal Canadiens in five games.

Although the Rangers would not reach the Finals again until 1994, they built a strong team with the likes of John Vanbiesbrouck, Brian Leetch, and Tony Granato. When Neil Smith was hired as general manager in 1989, he brought in superstar Mark Messier, and the Rangers would banish those shouts of "1940!"

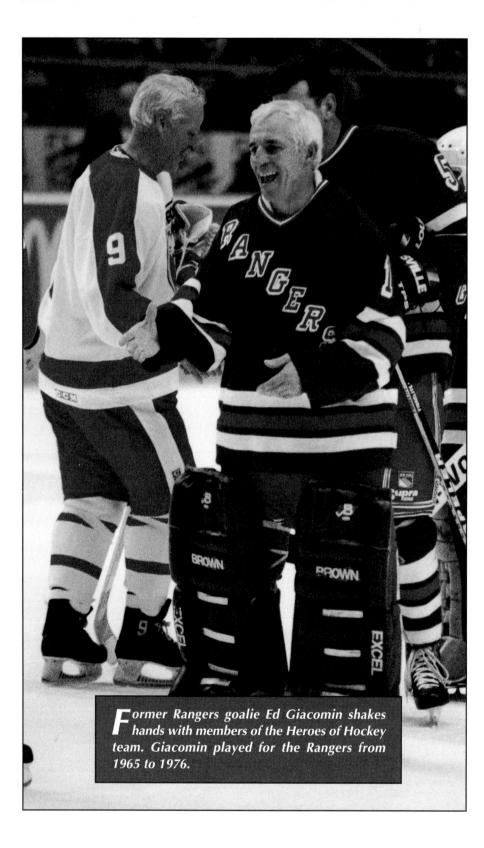

*F*ormer Rangers goalie Ed Giacomin shakes hands with members of the Heroes of Hockey team. Giacomin played for the Rangers from 1965 to 1976.

HONORABLE RANGERS

There have been many great players throughout the years, but few are as legendary as Brad Park, Rod Gilbert, and Ed Giacomin. These players left an impressive mark on the Rangers during the 1960s and 1970s. Three current players have done the same for the Rangers in the 1980s and 1990s: Brian Leetch, Mike Richter, and Mark Messier.

Brad Park

Defenseman Brad Park played for the Rangers from 1968–75. He was only twenty years old when he scored his first NHL goal early in his rookie season. He jumped ecstatically on the ice—and fell! Park's response was to grin and pick himself up.

Park was very popular with the fans, and he served as the Rangers' captain from 1974 through November 1975. During his career with the Rangers, he scored 95 goals and had 283 assists for a total of 378 points. He also holds the Rangers' record for most goals scored in one season by a defenseman (25 during the 1973–74 season.) However, Park's career with the Rangers came to an end in 1975 when New York traded him, along with Jean Ratelle and Joe Zanussi, to the Boston Bruins for Phil Esposito and Carol Vadnais. He went on to have a sterling career with Boston, and was elected to the Hockey Hall of Fame in 1988.

Rod Gilbert

Right-wing Rod Gilbert played for the Rangers between 1960 and 1978. He holds several records. He played the most seasons with the Rangers—eighteen. He also holds the record for most goals (406), most assists (615), and most points (1,021). For fourteen of those eighteen seasons, Gilbert scored thirty goals or more—another Rangers' record. He is second only to Brian Leetch in playoff scoring, with a total of 67 points. Gilbert's remarkable talents earned him a place in the Hall of Fame in 1982.

Ed Giacomin

Ed Giacomin displayed his amazing goaltending talents for the Rangers from 1965–76. He shares the record for most games played in one season (70) with goalie Johnny Bower (1953–54). More importantly, Giacomin holds the Rangers' record for most career wins (266) and most career shutouts (49). It's not surprising that Giacomin is also a Hall of Famer, having been elected in 1987.

Gliding in front of the goal crease, Rangers defenseman Brian Leetch tries to score on Sean Burke of the Hartford Whalers.

Brian Leetch

Defenseman Brian Leetch joined the Rangers in 1987, making his National Hockey League (NHL) debut on February 29, 1988, after playing in the Olympic Games in Calgary. He won the Calder Trophy as the League's Rookie of the Year in 1988–89, setting an NHL record for most goals by a rookie defenseman (23). He not only broke the Rangers' rookie records for most goals that season, but also for assists (48) and points (71).

Leetch's accomplishments have continued to this day. He collected his 500th assist during the 1996–97 season, earning him second place on the Rangers' all-time assist list. He also scored his 600th career NHL

Concentrating on the puck, Mike Richter makes sure he has deflected it away from the Rangers' net.

point, making him the Rangers' all-time scorer among defensemen. He has been named an All-Star player several times, and when not on the ice, he does charity work for the Leukemia Society and Ronald McDonald House.

Mike Richter

The efforts of goalie Mike Richter are just as spectacular. He made his NHL debut as the starting goalie for the Rangers in Game 4 of their first round playoff series in 1989 against Pittsburgh. Since then, he has had a remarkable career. During the 1993–94 season, he appeared in 68 games and won 42. That made him the first Rangers' goalie to lead the NHL in wins since Ed Giacomin led the league with 37 in 1968–69. During the 1996–97 season, he moved into fourth place on the Rangers' all-time wins list with his 158th win on December 1 against Montreal.

More importantly, Mike Richter has always been known for his generosity. In the past, he has won the Thurman Munson Award for his charitable work as well as the Sloan-Kettering Award of Courage for his work with the well-known cancer hospital.

Mark Messier

Then there is center Mark Messier, perhaps the one player who has had the greatest impact on the Rangers in recent history. He had already helped the Edmonton Oilers win five Stanley Cups before being acquired by the Rangers on October 4, 1991. Three days later, he made his debut as the Rangers' new captain. Three seasons later, he made headlines by guaranteeing a win in Game 6 of the Conference Finals against the New Jersey Devils. He then went on to score the winning goal in Game 7 of the Stanley Cup Finals against Vancouver, earning the Rangers their first Stanley Cup victory since 1940.

After the 1996–97 season, Messier opted to leave the Rangers, signing a three-year $20 million contract with the Vancouver Canucks.

There are certainly several other great players who have worn a Rangers' uniform. Still, there's no doubt that these legendary players are among the best the game has ever seen.

*O*ne of the greatest coaches in team history, Lester Patrick led the Rangers to two Stanley Cups—in 1928 and 1933.

RANGERS' LEADERS

Many legendary figures have had a hand in the success of the Rangers' franchise. However, these three men—Lester Patrick, Emile Francis, and Neil Smith—may have had the biggest impact.

Lester Patrick

Few men have left their mark on the Rangers as strongly as Coach Lester Patrick. He not only put together eleven winning teams between 1926–39, but he was also good at solving problems.

In 1928, the Rangers were playing the Montreal Maroons for the Stanley Cup. Montreal had already won the first game. The second game was tied 0–0 when Ranger goalie Lorne Chabot was injured and had to be taken to the hospital. In those days, teams couldn't afford to pay another salary to a second goalie who would spend most of his time sitting on the bench. Patrick wanted to ask Alex Connell, the Ottawa Senator goalie who happened to be sitting in the stands, to substitute for Chabot. However, Maroons coach Eddie Gerard would not give permission.

Patrick was furious. He had no goalie. Now what was he supposed to do?

Frank Boucher half jokingly suggested that Patrick himself play.[1]

To everyone's surprise, that's just what Patrick did. He was forty-four years old and had only played goal once in his hockey career. Still, he managed to keep Montreal scoreless for two periods. All of the Rangers tried to protect Patrick as much as they could. New York scored once, but then a Montreal forward slid the puck past a tired Patrick. The game went into overtime, but luckily Rangers forward Frank Boucher scored a second goal. Thanks to the quick-thinking Patrick, New York won the game, and ultimately the Stanley Cup!

Emile Francis

Lester Patrick coached a total of 604 games with 281 wins. That record earned him second place in the history of New York Rangers' coaches. First place belongs to Emile Francis. Francis had been a goalie during his playing days with the Chicago Black Hawks and the New York Rangers. He made up for his small size by being very quick, earning him the nickname "the Cat."[2] From 1965–75, Francis served as head coach three separate times. During his career, he

Rangers coach Emile Francis lets out a yell after his team scores a goal. Francis is the winningest coach in Rangers' history.

coached 654 games, winning 342 times. Under his reign, the Rangers rebuilt themselves. He acquired tough players such as Reg Fleming, Orland Kurtenbach, Don Simmons, and Red Berenson. He even persuaded right-wing Bernie "Boom Boom" Geoffrion to make a comeback. He also traded for goalie Ed Giacomin and helped turn him into a star.

Francis's efforts paid off. Beginning with the 1966–67 season, the Rangers made the playoffs nine consecutive seasons—the only NHL team of the period to accomplish that feat. He worked his players hard, but he always treated them with respect. He was careful not to criticize a player in front of the sportswriters. He worked long hours and always kept

General Manager Neil Smith, (rear), and Coach Colin Campbell watch a Rangers' practice. Many people credit Smith with the Rangers' rise to the top of the NHL.

his office clock twenty minutes ahead of the actual time. "It sets the tempo for our club," Francis would say. "Fast, and slightly ahead of schedule."[3] Through his hard work, the popular coach helped lift his team out of the dismal 1950s and into a new winning era.

Neil Smith

Neil Smith has done the same thing for the Rangers in the present day. In his first three seasons after joining the club as general manager in 1989, New York finished in first place twice and second place once. That was the best three consecutive finishes in the club's history. In honor of his accomplishments, Smith was named the NHL Executive of the Year by *The Sporting News* for 1992. He was the first Rangers' executive to ever win that award. He was also promoted to the position of president and general manager.

Under his skillful guidance, the Rangers' lineup improved dramatically. He acquired outstanding players such as Mark Messier, Jeff Beukeboom, Glenn Healy, and Kevin Lowe. However, his greatest and most daring acquisitions came at a crucial time. On March 21, 1994, just before the deadline, he made trades to acquire Craig MacTavish, Brian Noonan, Glenn Anderson, and Stephane Matteau. Less than three short months later, the incredible team that Smith helped to create went on to win the fourth Stanley Cup in franchise history. That team also set a club record with 52 wins and 112 points. For all his efforts, Neil Smith was named the *Hockey News'* Executive of the Year.

The great coaches and managers of the New York Rangers may have had different styles and ideas, but they had one thing in common. They helped put together the right combination of players to help the team reach its potential. What happens on the ice may be fun to watch—but it wouldn't be possible without the hard work of great coaches and managers working behind the scenes.

*F*orwards Bill Cook (left) and Fred "Bun" Cook (right), along with center Frank Boucher, were three of the greatest Rangers from the team's early years.

GREAT SEASONS

Most hockey clubs take years to develop talent, but not the New York Rangers. Thanks to the efforts of Constantine F. K. Smythe, the Rangers' first manager, New York's newest hockey team quickly hired some impressive players.

The Early Years

George Lewis "Tex" Rickard was the owner of the Rangers. Of course, he wanted to fill the seats of Madison Square Garden with thousands of paying fans. So Smythe was forced to hire the best, mostly highly paid professionals rather than amateurs. He quickly hired three memorable players. First there was Murray Murdoch, who was nicknamed the "Iron Man." He never missed a game in eleven seasons as a Ranger. Then there was Ivan "Ching" Johnson, a big, bald player known for his toughness. And then there was Clarence "Taffy" Abel, who became Johnson's defensive partner.

Smythe also acquired three key forwards who would become one of the league's top lines and remain so for the next ten years: center Frank Boucher and two brothers—Bill and Fred "Bun" Cook. In 1927, this fine cast of players helped the Rangers win the five-team American Division handily with a record of 25–13–6 for 56 points, 11 ahead of the Boston Bruins. Winger Bill Cook led the league with 33 goals and won the Art Ross Trophy as the NHL's top scorer in the 1926–27 season. Although they were eliminated by the Bruins in the first round of the playoffs, the Rangers were a big hit with the fans. It didn't take long for the team to earn a new nickname: "The Broadway Blueshirts . . . The Classiest Team in Hockey."[1]

Boucher and the Cook Brothers

Eighteen months after making their debut, the Rangers won the Stanley Cup. They would end up going to the Finals four times in six years. Center Frank Boucher was often among the leaders in assists. He won the Lady Byng Memorial Trophy for sportsmanship seven times—so often, in fact, that the league let him keep the award! He played for the Rangers during the 1937–38 season, scoring 152 goals. In 1940, he became the Rangers' coach. During the next eight years, he coached 525 games and, including the playoffs, won 179 of them.

Bill Cook won a second scoring title during the 1932–33 season, and in April, his overtime goal in Game 4 of the Finals gave the Rangers a 1–0 win over Toronto and their second Stanley Cup title.

The New York Rangers Hockey Team

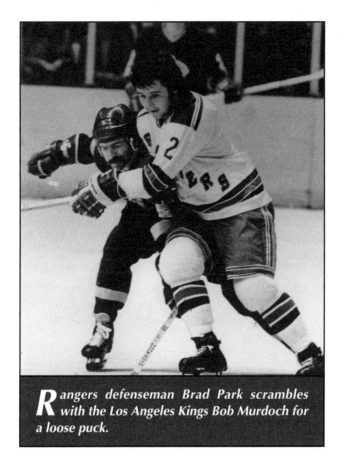

*R*angers defenseman Brad Park scrambles with the Los Angeles Kings Bob Murdoch for a loose puck.

Fred "Bun" Cook wore a blueshirt through the 1935–36 season, scoring a total of 154 goals. These three players were the heart of the Rangers' team. Although several great players would follow, Rangers' fans wouldn't see another great line of forwards until the early 1970s.

The G-A-G Line

In 1971, winger Vic Hadfield had already been a Ranger for ten years. He had averaged just 16 goals a year. Then manager and coach Emile "the Cat" Francis put

A dam Graves raises his arm in celebration after teammate Mark Messier scored the tying goal in Game 6 of the 1994 Eastern Conference Finals against the New Jersey Devils.

him on a line with center Jean Ratelle and right-wing Rod Gilbert. Hadfield exploded during the 1971–72 season, scoring 50 goals and 106 points. That was the first time that a Ranger had ever scored 50 goals.

Meanwhile, Ratelle collected 109 points—a club record—on 46 goals and 63 assists. Rod Gilbert collected 97 points on 43 goals and 54 assists. Together, these three players became known as the G-A-G (Goal-a-Game) Line.[2] The G-A-G line helped the Rangers reach the Finals for the eighth time in their history. They beat Montreal and Chicago in the first two rounds, but lost to the powerful Bruins in the Stanley Cup Finals.

Defenseman Brad Park was another key player during that memorable season. He was only twenty-four years old, and suffered knee and ankle injuries throughout his career. Yet in the 1971–72 season, he scored 24 goals and compiled 73 points.

The Magic of '94

The 1993–94 season was filled with drama as a result of the play of Brian Leetch, Mark Messier, and Mike Richter. After trailing 3–2 against the New Jersey Devils in the Stanley Cup playoffs, a defiant Messier proclaimed "We'll Win Tonight." That statement made all the headlines before Game 6.

The Rangers trailed 2–0 in the final two minutes of the second period. That's when Messier moved across the Devils' blue line and passed the puck to forward Alexei Kovalev. Goal!

At 2:49 into the third period, Messier scored a goal to tie the game at 2–2. Kovalev then picked up the puck near the center ice line and slipped a pass to Brian Leetch. As Leetch skated by Kovalev, he slid the puck back to Kovalev, who blasted the puck toward Devils goalie Martin Brodeur. Brodeur deflected it, but Mark Messier was there to swat the puck. Another goal! The Rangers now led 3–2, and when it was all over, the Rangers would score one more goal to decisively win Game 6.

Thanks to the heroic efforts of Leetch and Messier in the third period, as well as superb goaltending by Mike Richter, the Rangers were able to go on to defeat Vancouver to win the Stanley Cup after fifty-four long years.

*P*rior to the 1996–97 season, the Rangers added Wayne Gretzky—the league's all-time leading scorer—to their roster.

LOOKING TO THE FUTURE

nfortunately, not all has gone well for the Rangers since that remarkable Stanley Cup victory in 1994. Coach Mike Keenan moved on to coach the St. Louis Blues. Rangers' fans were bitter about his departure for two reasons. Before the Stanley Cup's seventh game, Keenan denied any interest in leaving New York. Also, at the victory parade, Keenan once again repeated his pledge to remain with the Rangers. Many Rangers' fans believed him. Now they considered him a traitor. Keenan wasn't as lucky with the St. Louis Blues. He was eventually fired in 1997.

The Rangers replaced Keenan with assistant coach Colin Campbell. In 1995, the Rangers were overpowered by Philadelphia, 4–0, in the second round of the playoffs. In 1996, they lost again in the second round, this time to the Pittsburgh Penguins.

The Great One Comes Aboard

The 1996–97 season was filled with both promise and disappointment. Wayne Gretzky, Mark Messier's longtime friend with the Edmonton Oilers, joined the Rangers amid much publicity. He played his first game in a Rangers' uniform on October 5, 1996.

With the great Wayne Gretzky and Mark Messier together again, the Rangers played well in the post-season. They beat both the Florida Panthers and the New Jersey Devils before losing to the Philadelphia Flyers in the Eastern Conference Finals.

The future looks bright for the Rangers. President and General Manager Neil Smith remains at the Rangers' helm. He is the type of leader who doesn't knock his players or members of his staff. He is very positive in his approach.

One of the players Smith hopes to keep for a long time is goalie Mike Richter. He has been reliable in the regular season and terrific in the postseason. A goalie is a team's biggest impact player. He's the last line of defense, someone who can make up for mistakes made by the five other guys in front of him. And Smith knows that.

". . . I think Mike Richter is a great goalie," says Neil Smith. "When you just start with those three—a great goalie, a great leader in Mess (Mark Messier), and a Norris Trophy caliber defenseman (Brian Leetch)—that's a great start."[1]

The Rangers also have to make sure that defense-man Brian Leetch is kept in a New York uniform. The Rangers cannot go far in postseason unless they have

*J*eff Beukeboom of New York knocks the Tampa Bay Lightning's Rob Zamuner to the ice after a devastating body check.

a healthy Leetch. Born in 1969, Leetch should have several more great years ahead of him.

Leetch is the player who directs the offense, and keeps opposing goal scorers from camping in front of the Rangers' net to have easy scoring opportunities. When he has the puck behind the net, Leetch is one of the best at bringing the puck up the ice.

When the Rangers slump on the power play, it is Leetch who creates and makes a big play to spark the New York offense. Leetch, now the team's captain, is the rock in front of Richter, and the man who calms his teammates when everything seems to go wrong.

Leetch still has possibly another ten years to play. Richter is likely to play for another six or seven, while

The Rangers Alexei Kovalev wards off Ray Ferraro of the New York Islanders. The Rangers are counting on Kovalev to become one of the league's brightest stars.

Gretzky's career is winding down. Messier left the team after the 1996–97 season to sign with the Vancouver Canucks.

The Core Group

Two other players the Rangers could rely on in the future are defenseman Jeff Beukeboom and forward Adam Graves. Beukeboom, born in 1965, is not a very flashy player but works hard.

Beukeboom does not receive the press that the other players do, but he is just as important. When Leetch is rushing up the ice, it is Beukeboom who has to make sure he stays back to protect Richter from any breakaways. When an opponent tries to slide around Beukeboom, he will crush the opponent into the boards, stopping the attempt to score on Richter.

Like Beukeboom, Adam Graves has become a very reliable player and a fan favorite because of his hard work. Graves never shouts to the press that he is not getting enough attention. Graves is a player who will stick up for a smaller player when it is necessary. He does what hockey players refer to as "dirty work." This means that he is the player responsible for going to the boards and digging out the puck. He is responsible for trying to get the puck to players in shooting position and planting himself in front of the net to distract the other team's goaltender. These types of responsibilities are rarely noticed by the average fan, nor are they publicized heavily in the newspapers.

One of the bright young stars of the future is right-wing Alexei Kovalev. Born in 1973, Kovalev is a highly skilled player who has at times shown flashes of brilliance. Unfortunately, he's been injured several times. If he can stay healthy, Kovalev will certainly play a big role in seasons to come.

The future of the Rangers depends on the management and players. There is youth and skill in both. It will be up to both to strive for the same goal in future years—to win another Stanley Cup.

STATISTICS

Team Record

The Rangers NHL History

SEASONS	W	L	T	PCT	STANLEY CUPS
1926–27 to 1929–30	82	59	35	.565	1928
1930–31 to 1939–40	226	168	82	.561	1933, 1940
1940–41 to 1941–50	180	283	83	.406	None
1950–51 to 1959–60	239	319	142	.443	None
1960–61 to 1969–70	278	322	116	.469	None
1970–71 to 1979–80	387	288	117	.563	None
1980–81 to 1989–90	351	347	102	.503	None
1990–91 to 1996–97	273	203	64	.565	1994

The Rangers Today

SEASON	W	L	T	PCT	COACH	DIVISION FINISH
1990–91	36	31	13	.531	Roger Neilson	2nd Patrick
1991–92	50	25	5	.656	Roger Neilson	1st Patrick
1992–93	34	39	11	.470	Roger Neilson Ron Smith	6th Patrick
1993–94	52	24	8	.667	Mike Keenan	1st Atlantic
1994–95	22	23	3	.490	Colin Campbell	4th Atlantic
1995–96	41	27	14	.585	Colin Campbell	2nd Atlantic
1996–97	38	34	10	.524	Colin Campbell	4th Atlantic

Total History

W	L	T	PCT	STANLEY CUPS
2,016	1,989	741	.503	4

W=Wins   **T**=Ties   **STANLEY CUPS**=Stanley
L=Losses   **PCT**=Winning Percentage   Cups won

Championship Coaches

| COACH | REGULAR SEASON | | | POSTSEASON | | STANLEY CUPS |
	W	L	T	W	L	
Lester Patrick	281	216	107	31	26	1928, 1933
Frank Boucher	166	243	77	13	14	1940
Mike Keenan	52	24	8	16	7	1994

Great Skaters

PLAYER	SEA	CAREER STATISTICS				
		YRS	GAMES	G	A	PTS
Frank Boucher	1926–38 1943–44	14	557	161	262	423
Bill Cook	1926–37	11	452	223	132	355
Rod Gilbert	1960–78	18	1,065	406	615	1,021
Adam Graves	1991–	10	676	209	204	413
Vic Hadfield	1961–74	16	1,002	323	389	712
Harry Howell	1952–69	21	1,411	94	324	418
Brian Leetch	1987–	10	649	147	503	650
Mark Messier	1991–97	18	1,272	575	977	1,552
Brad Park	1968–75	17	1,113	213	683	896
Jean Ratelle	1960–75	21	1,070	252	420	672

SEA=Seasons with Rangers **GAMES**=Games Played **A**=Assists
YRS=Years in the NHL **G**=Goals **PTS**=Points Scored

Great Goalies

PLAYER	SEA	CAREER STATISTICS					
		YRS	GAMES	MIN	GA	SH	GAA
Ed Giacomin	1965–76	13	610	35,693	1,675	54	2.82
Dave Kerr	1934–41	11	426	26,519	960	51	2.17
Mike Richter	1989–	8	352	20,015	978	18	2.93
John Vanbiesbrouck	1981–82 1983–93	15	657	37,432	1,959	25	3.14
Gump Worsley	1952–63	21	862	50,232	2,432	43	2.90

SEA=Seasons with Rangers **MIN**=Minutes Played **GAA**=Goals Against Average
YRS=Years in the NHL **GA**=Goals Against
GAMES=Games Played **SH**=Shutouts

The New York Rangers Hockey Team

CHAPTER NOTES

Chapter 2

1. Michael L. LaBlanc, ed., *Professional Sports Team Histories: Hockey* (Gale Research, 1994), p. 63.
2. Ibid., p. 66.

Chapter 4

1. Michael L. LaBlanc, ed., *Professional Sports Team Histories: Hockey* (Gale Research, 1994), p. 67.
2. Charles Moritz, ed., *Current Biography Yearbook, 1968* (H. W. Wilson Company, 1968, 1969), p. 130.
3. Ibid., p. 132.

Chapter 5

1. Michael L. LaBlanc, ed., *Professional Sports Team Histories: Hockey* (Gale Research, 1994), p. 66.
2. Ibid., p. 76.

Chapter 6

1. Neil Smith, interview by John Dellapina, *Newsday*, May 14, 1996.

GLOSSARY

assist—The action of a player, usually a pass, that allows a teammate to score a goal.

blue lines—The two lines on the ice that mark the beginning of the offensive zones.

boards—The low wall surrounding the hockey rink.

cage—Another term for the goal net.

center—The job of the center is usually to set up the wingers for shots.

defenseman—The players whose main job is to stop the opposing team's forwards from getting good shots on goal.

faceoff—A method in which two opponents attempt to gain control of the puck, which is dropped by the referee.

forecheck—To check an opponent while he is still in his defensive zone.

forward—One of the three players that line up closest to the other team's goal. The forwards are also known as the right-wing, the left-wing, and the center.

goalie—The player whose main responsibility is to stay in front of the net and deflect away or block the opposing team's shots.

holding—A penalty given out when a player holds an opponent and interferes with the opponent's ability to move freely.

lines—Arrangements of three forwards or two defensemen who go out on to the ice to play for shifts of roughly two minutes.

overtime—The time added on to a game if the three regulation periods end in a tie score. The overtime is five minutes long in the regular season. In the postseason, the teams play until someone scores.

The New York Rangers Hockey Team

period—A twenty-minute span of time. There are three periods in a standard hockey game.

point—A player is given a point whenever that person scores a goal or records an assist.

power play—A situation in which one team temporarily has an extra player (or players) on the ice because of a penalty on the other team.

pull—The act of taking the goalie off of the ice to get an extra skater for an attacking situation.

red line—The line that marks center ice.

slap shot—A shot in which players raise their sticks off the ice and bring them back to about waist height, and then shoot the puck after the windup.

Stanley Cup—The trophy presented annually to the NHL's championship team.

wrist shot—A type of shot where players get velocity by leaving their stick on the ice and snapping their wrists.

FURTHER READING

Everson, Mark. *New York Rangers*. Mankato, Minn.: Creative Education, Inc., 1995.

Fortunato, Frank. *Wayne Gretzky: Star Center*. Springfield, N.J.: Enslow Publishers, Inc., 1998.

Knapp, Ron. *Top 10 Hockey Scorers*. Springfield, N.J.: Enslow Publishers, Inc., 1994.

Krieser, John, and Lou Friedman. *The New York Rangers: Broadway on Ice*. Champaign, Ill.: Sagamore Publishing, Incorporated, 1996.

Meisel, Barry. *Losing the Edge: The Rise & Fall of Stanley Cup Champion New York Rangers*. New York: Simon & Schuster Trade, 1995.

Mekz, Andrew K. *Rangers Wit: Reflections, Retorts & Reminiscences from the Stanley Cup Champs*. ed. Anne E. Broussard. Swarthmore, Pa.: Wit Press, 1994.

Rappoport, Ken. *Sports Great Wayne Gretzky*. Springfield, N.J.: Enslow Publishers, Inc., 1996.

Sullivan, Michael J. *Mark Messier: Star Center*. Springfield, N.J.: Enslow Publishers, Inc., 1997.

INDEX

WHERE TO WRITE

New York Rangers
2 Penn Plaza
14th Floor
New York, NY 10121

WEBSITE

http://www.nhl.com/teams/nyr/index.htm